Copyright © 2021
All Rights Reserved.

No part of this publication may be reproduced, distributed or transmitted in any form or by any means including photocopying, recording or other electronic or mechanical methods, without permission of the publisher, except in the case of brief quotations embodied in critical reviews and certain other non-commercial uses permitted by copyright law.

ALL RIGHTS RESERVED

ALL RIGHTS RESERVED

ALL RIGHTS RESERVED

ALL RIGHTS RESERVED

ALL RIGHTS RESERVED

ALL RIGHTS RESERVED

ALL RIGHTS RESERVED

ALL RIGHTS RESERVED

ALL RIGHTS RESERVED

ALL RIGHTS RESERVED

ALL RIGHTS RESERVED

ALL RIGHTS RESERVED

ALL RIGHTS RESERVED

ALL RIGHTS RESERVED

ALL RIGHTS RESERVED

ALL RIGHTS RESERVED

ALL RIGHTS RESERVED

ALL RIGHTS RESERVED

ALL RIGHTS RESERVED

ALL RIGHTS RESERVED

ALL RIGHTS RESERVED

ALL RIGHTS RESERVED

ALL RIGHTS RESERVED

ALL RIGHTS RESERVED

ALL RIGHTS RESERVED

ALL RIGHTS RESERVED

ALL RIGHTS RESERVED

ALL RIGHTS RESERVED

ALL RIGHTS RESERVED

ALL RIGHTS RESERVED

ALL RIGHTS RESERVED

ALL RIGHTS RESERVED

ALL RIGHTS RESERVED

Made in the USA
Columbia, SC
20 May 2025

58209577R00037